PAUL ROMANUK

HOCKEY
SUPERSTARS
2021-2022

Your complete guide to the 2021–2022 season,
featuring action photos of
your favorite players

SCHOLASTIC
TORONTO NEW YORK LONDON AUCKLAND SYDNEY
MEXICO CITY NEW DELHI HONG KONG BUENOS AIRES

THE TEAMS

WESTERN CONFERENCE — PACIFIC DIVISION

CALGARY FLAMES
team colors: red, gold, black and white
home arena: Scotiabank Saddledome
mascot: Harvey the Hound
Stanley Cups won: 1

EDMONTON OILERS
team colors: white, royal blue and orange
home arena: Rogers Place
mascot: Hunter
Stanley Cups won: 5

ANAHEIM DUCKS
team colors: black, gold, orange and silver
home arena: Honda Center
mascot: Wild Wing
Stanley Cups won: 1

LOS ANGELES KINGS
team colors: white, black and silver
home arena: Staples Center
mascot: Bailey
Stanley Cups won: 2

SEATTLE KRAKEN
team colors: dark blue, medium blue, light blue and red
home arena: Climate Pledge Arena

VANCOUVER CANUCKS
team colors: blue, silver, green and white
home arena: Rogers Arena
mascot: Fin

SAN JOSE SHARKS
team colors: teal, black, orange and white
home arena: SAP Center at San Jose
mascot: S.J. Sharkie

VEGAS GOLDEN KNIGHTS
team colors: steel gray, gold, red and black
home arena: T-Mobile Arena
mascot: Chance

WESTERN CONFERENCE — CENTRAL DIVISION

CHICAGO BLACKHAWKS
nickname: Hawks
team colors: red, black and white
home arena: United Center
mascot: Tommy Hawk
Stanley Cups won: 6

COLORADO AVALANCHE
nickname: Avs
team colors: burgundy, silver, black, blue and white
home arena: Pepsi Center
mascot: Bernie
Stanley Cups won: 2

DALLAS STARS
team colors: green, white, black and silver
home arena: American Airlines Center
mascot: Victor E. Green
Stanley Cups won: 1

NASHVILLE PREDATORS
nickname: Preds
team colors: dark blue, white and gold
home arena: Bridgestone Arena
mascot: Gnash

ARIZONA COYOTES
team colors: red, black and sand
home arena: Gila River Arena
mascot: Howler

MINNESOTA WILD
team colors: red, green, gold, wheat and white
home arena: Xcel Energy Center
mascot: Nordy

WINNIPEG JETS
team colors: dark blue, blue, gray, silver, red and white
home arena: Canada Life Centre
mascot: Mick E. Moose

ST. LOUIS BLUES
team colors: blue, gold, dark blue and white
home arena: Enterprise Center
mascot: Louie
Stanley Cups won: 1

EASTERN CONFERENCE – ATLANTIC DIVISION

TORONTO MAPLE LEAFS
nickname: Leafs
team colors: blue and white
home arena: Scotiabank Arena
mascot: Carlton the Bear
Stanley Cups won: 11

. . . .

BUFFALO SABRES
team colors: navy blue, gold and silver
home arena: KeyBank Center
mascot: Sabretooth

. . . .

FLORIDA PANTHERS
nickname: Cats
team colors: red, navy blue and gold
home arena: BB&T Center
mascots: Stanley C. Panther and Viktor E. Ratt

OTTAWA SENATORS
nickname: Sens
team colors: black, red, gold and white
home arena: Canadian Tire Centre
mascot: Spartacat

. . . .

TAMPA BAY LIGHTNING
nickname: Bolts
team colors: blue, black and white
home arena: Amalie Arena
mascot: ThunderBug
Stanley Cups won: 3

MONTREAL CANADIENS
nickname: Habs
team colors: red, blue and white
home arena: Bell Centre
mascot: Youppi
Stanley Cups won: 24

. . . .

DETROIT RED WINGS
nickname: Wings
team colors: red and white
home arena: Little Caesars Arena
mascot (unofficial): Al the Octopus
Stanley Cups won: 11

. . . .

BOSTON BRUINS
nickname: Bs
team colors: gold, black and white
home arena: TD Garden
mascot: Blades
Stanley Cups won: 6

EASTERN CONFERENCE – METROPOLITAN DIVISION

NEW YORK RANGERS
nickname: Blueshirts
team colors: blue, white and red
home arena: Madison Square Garden
Stanley Cups won: 4

. . . .

COLUMBUS BLUE JACKETS
nickname: Jackets
team colors: blue, red and silver
home arena: Nationwide Arena
mascot: Stinger

. . . .

WASHINGTON CAPITALS
nickname: Caps
team colors: red, navy blue and white
home arena: Capital One Arena
mascot: Slapshot
Stanley Cups won: 1

NEW YORK ISLANDERS
nickname: Isles
team colors: orange, blue and white
home arena: UBS Arena
mascot: Sparky the Dragon
Stanley Cups won: 4

. . . .

PITTSBURGH PENGUINS
nickname: Pens
team colors: black, gold and white
home arena: PPG Paints Arena
mascot: Iceburgh
Stanley Cups won: 5

PHILADELPHIA FLYERS
team colors: orange, white and black
home arena: Wells Fargo Center
mascot: Gritty
Stanley Cups won: 2

. . . .

NEW JERSEY DEVILS
team colors: red, black and white
home arena: Prudential Center
mascot: N.J. Devil
Stanley Cups won: 3

. . . .

CAROLINA HURRICANES
nickname: Canes
team colors: red, black, gray and white
home arena: PNC Arena
mascots: Stormy and Caroline
Stanley Cups won: 1

YOUR FAVORITE TEAM

Name of your favorite team: _____

Conference and division: _____

Players on your favorite team at the start of the season:

Number	Name	Position
_____	_____	_____
_____	_____	_____
_____	_____	_____
_____	_____	_____
_____	_____	_____
_____	_____	_____
_____	_____	_____
_____	_____	_____
_____	_____	_____
_____	_____	_____
_____	_____	_____
_____	_____	_____
_____	_____	_____
_____	_____	_____

Changes, Trades, New Players

_____   _____   _____
_____   _____   _____
_____   _____   _____
_____   _____   _____
_____   _____   _____
_____   _____   _____
_____   _____   _____

End-of-Season Standings

Fill in the name of the team you think will finish in first place in each of the four NHL divisions.

WESTERN CONFERENCE

_____   **PACIFIC DIVISION**

_____   **CENTRAL DIVISION**

EASTERN CONFERENCE

ATLANTIC DIVISION   _____

METROPOLITAN DIVISION   _____

The Playoffs

Which two teams will meet in the Stanley Cup Final? Fill in their names below, then circle the team you think will win.

Eastern Conference Winner: _____

Western Conference Winner: _____

YOUR FAVORITE TEAM

Your Team — All Season Long

The standings of hockey teams are listed at NHL.com and on the sports pages of the newspaper all season long. The standings will show you which team is in first place, second place, etc., right down to last place.

Some of the abbreviations you'll become familiar with are: GP for games played; W for wins; L for losses; OT for overtime losses; PTS for points; A for assists; G for goals.

Check the standings on the same day of every month and copy down what they say about your team. By keeping track of your team this way you'll be able to see when it was playing well and when it wasn't.

	GP	W	L	OT	PTS
NOVEMBER 1					
DECEMBER 1					
JANUARY 1					
FEBRUARY 1					
MARCH 1					
APRIL 1					
MAY 1					

Final Standings

At the end of the season print the final record of your team below.

YOUR TEAM	GP	W	L	OT	PTS

Your Favorite Players' Scoring Records

While you're keeping track of your favorite team during the season, you can also follow the progress of your favorite players. Just fill in their point totals on the same day of every month.

player	nov 1	dec 1	jan 1	feb 1	mar 1	apr 1	may 1

Your Favorite Goaltenders' Records

You can keep track of your favorite goaltenders' averages during the season. Just fill in the information below.

GAA is the abbreviation for goals-against average. That's the average number of goals given up by a goaltender during a game over the course of the season.

goaltender	nov 1	dec 1	jan 1	feb 1	mar 1	apr 1	may 1

CALGARY FLAMES

Last season was a big step forward for Calgary defenseman Rasmus Andersson. He was on the ice far more than in previous seasons, and in more crucial situations. Rasmus's time on ice (TOI) average went from 19:56 during the 2019–2020 season to 21:13 last season, and his TOI during power plays more than doubled, to 2:44. Rasmus also benefited from playing most of the season alongside Calgary's top defenseman, veteran Mark Giordano.

"I think Rasmus benefits from being around Gio on the ice and off the ice," said Flames assistant coach Ryan Huska. "Rasmus is a smart guy, very astute, and I think he pays attention to what's going on around him. When he has a guy like Mark, who he can learn a lot about leadership from, I think that's important."

> "It's one of those things where it has to be fun to be here [the NHL]. You have to enjoy it. If it's not going to be fun here, it's not going to be fun anywhere."

It's nothing new for Rasmus to learn a lot by watching and listening. His dad, Peter, was a superstar defenseman in the Swedish Elitserien, then coached in Sweden and Switzerland. As a boy, Rasmus spent a lot of time tagging along with his dad while he was at work.

"I remember being a kid and running around the rink . . . I just wanted to be there every day," recalls Rasmus. "I had so much fun at the rink and seeing that my dad worked in hockey, and I thought it was the coolest thing ever. I wanted to grow up and be a professional hockey player."

That desire took Rasmus to Barrie, Ontario, to play in the Ontario Hockey League and then to Calgary's American Hockey League club. It was in the AHL that he started to realize what it would take to make the NHL.

"I think we all knew the kind of ability he had," said Huska, who also coached Rasmus in the AHL. "He just had to mature between the ears. He had to believe that he was an NHL player."

He certainly plays like he believes it now. He is confident, skilled and maturing into one of the best defensemen in the league.

DID YOU KNOW?

During the 2015–2016 season, playing in the OHL with the Barrie Colts, Rasmus led the league in points by a defenseman (9 goals, 51 assists, 60 points). He is the only Swedish-born player in league history to have accomplished that feat.

HOCKEY MEMORIES

Rasmus's pro debut came in October 2012 with the Swedish club Malmö Redhawks. He was 16. The game was against Örebro HK, where his father was head coach! His dad's team ended up winning, but Rasmus still calls it "probably my greatest hockey memory."

2020–2021 STATS

GP	G	A	PTS
56	5	16	21

Calgary Flames' 1st choice, 53rd overall, in 2015 NHL Entry Draft
1st NHL Team, Season: Calgary Flames, 2018–2019
Born: October 27, 1996, in Malmö, Sweden
Plays: Defense
Shoots: Right
Height: 1.85 m (6'1")
Weight: 97 kg (214 lbs.)

NICKLAS BACKSTROM

Nicklas Backstrom reached a couple of big personal milestones last season — 1000 career games and 700 career assists. As he heads into his 15th NHL season, it's as good a time as any to ask the question: Is Nicklas Backstrom the greatest Swedish forward to ever play in the NHL? There is certainly plenty of competition: Mats Sundin, Daniel Alfredsson and Daniel and Henrik Sedin all have more career points. Peter Forsberg has fewer points, but like Nicklas, he has his name on the Cup. There are many opinions — but what is undisputed is that Nicklas is a true superstar.

"Of the time I've been here, he's the guy who just never seems to have a down year or a bad stretch," says teammate John Carlson. "He just always seems on his game."

"He's been such an important piece of this organization for so many years, and to take a moment to honor him for what he's done and what he's accomplished I think is important," says Caps head coach Peter Laviolette.

"I think I'll appreciate these things more when I retire," says Nicklas. "I'll look back at the things that I've accomplished. But, right now, it's a nice number that you have to take and then just move on."

Many of Nicklas's assists have come on goals scored by his longtime friend, sometimes linemate and usual power-play partner Alex Ovechkin. When you share the stage with the greatest pure goal scorer of the era, maybe some of what you have accomplished gets a little overshadowed. But that's all good with Nicklas.

"After you've won, I think you're kind of in that mindset where you realize that it's doable. You kind of know what it takes and what kind of price you have to pay."

"I like it that way," says Nicklas. "He deserves all the credit. He's such a good goal scorer and such a great player . . . I'm just going to try and do my job. That's the way it's been and that's the way I want it to be."

So, is Nicklas Backstrom the greatest Swedish-born forward in NHL history? It's a fair question. The answer is: Probably not right now. But by the time he hangs up his skates, there's a decent chance he will be.

DID YOU KNOW?

When Nicklas played his 1000th game, his teammates formed a stick tunnel for him to walk through as he came out onto the ice, and all of the Caps players wore sweaters with Nic's number 19 for the pre-game warm-up.

HOCKEY MEMORIES

Nicklas's father tells a story about young Nicklas getting a pair of hand-me-down skates from his brother. He put them on and walked around inside the house, then he went outside and walked around on the driveway. At the end of the day his parents had to let him wear the skates to bed!

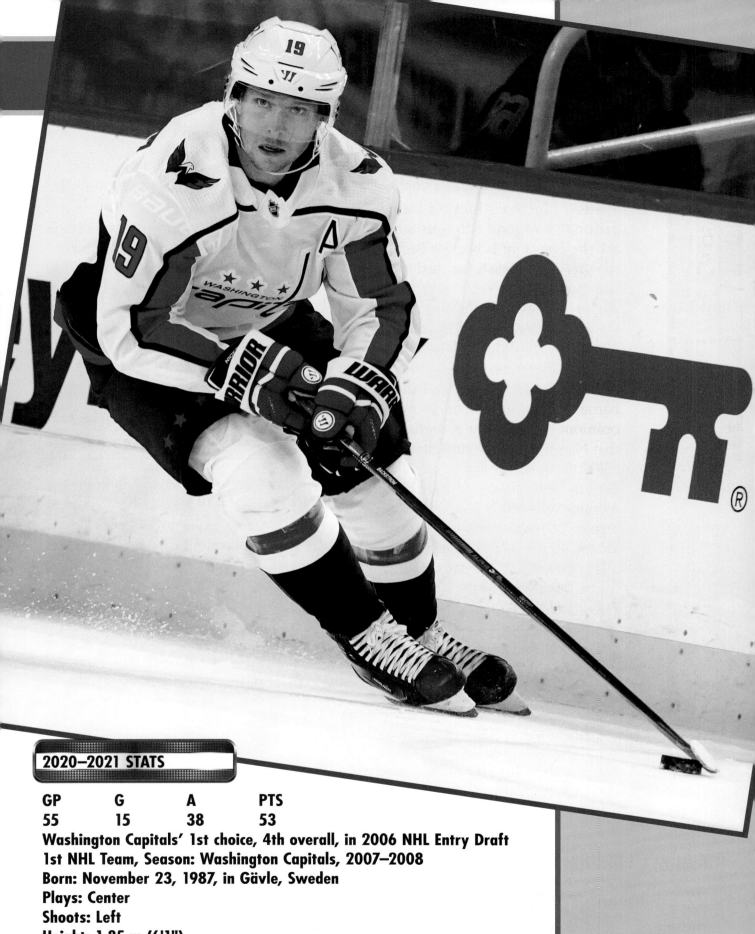

2020–2021 STATS

GP	G	A	PTS
55	15	38	53

Washington Capitals' 1st choice, 4th overall, in 2006 NHL Entry Draft
1st NHL Team, Season: Washington Capitals, 2007–2008
Born: November 23, 1987, in Gävle, Sweden
Plays: Center
Shoots: Left
Height: 1.85 m (6'1")
Weight: 93.5 kg (206 lbs.)

BROCK BOESER

Although actual total goals and points didn't reflect it because of the pandemic-shortened season, it was clear to anyone who watched the Canucks play a lot last season that Brock Boeser had returned to the form that saw him just miss out on winning the Calder Trophy as NHL Rookie of the Year in 2017–2018. Brock finished up with 23 goals, 26 assists and 49 points and led the Canucks in scoring. He hadn't topped the Vancouver scoring race since his rookie season, when he finished tied with Daniel Sedin. But as much as Brock's play was good news for Vancouver fans, the team didn't have a great season. The Canucks struggled in the North Division, out of the playoff picture. So, while Brock may have been happy with his own play, he would have traded some personal success for a little more team success.

"I just felt like I needed to get back to my game . . . not overthinking things and just playing off instinct."

"It's been a good year for me personally, but I'm not too worried about that," said Brock. "I just want to win hockey games and help produce for our team in any way I can, even if I'm not getting points or scoring goals. I want to make sure that I'm doing all of the little things right and doing all I can to help the team win."

One of those "little things" — his defensive play — was an area where Brock really worked hard to improve. That hard work led to him getting more ice time in important situations where the team needed to defend, rather than score.

"You kind of realize that when you play better defensively, then you get into the offensive zone cleaner and get more puck control," said Brock.

The Canucks have some of the best young talent in the NHL in Brock, Elias Pettersson and Quinn Hughes. They also have some good veteran players in the mix. You have to think it will all come together sooner than later.

DID YOU KNOW?
As a rookie with the University of North Dakota Fighting Hawks, Brock helped lead his team to an NCAA championship, scoring once and adding three assists in the championship game against the Quinnipiac Bobcats.

HOCKEY MEMORIES
"I started playing hockey when I was two. My earliest hockey memory is playing Mites when I was younger, and loving going to the rink every day and trying to chase my dream."

2020–2021 STATS

GP	G	A	PTS
56	23	26	49

Vancouver Canucks' 1st choice, 23rd overall, in 2015 NHL Entry Draft
1st NHL Team, Season: Vancouver Canucks, 2017–2018
Born: February 25, 1997, in Burnsville, Minnesota
Position: Right Wing
Shoots: Right
Height: 1.85 m (6'1")
Weight: 94.5 kg (208 lbs.)

NIKOLAJ EHLERS

There was a time when Winnipeg superstar Nikolaj Ehlers saw himself becoming a great soccer player. As a boy in Denmark, he was a highly regarded prospect in the national team program. But at age 14, he stepped out of the sport to concentrate full-time on hockey.

> **"The support that we get is great. And the city itself . . . everyone loves hockey, I love hockey, so it's a perfect fit for me."**

"I was playing on a [soccer] team when we were living in Switzerland," recalls Ehlers, "and the team I was playing for said I had to choose between hockey and soccer. For me, it wasn't a difficult choice."

So it was hockey full-time, and by 2013–2014 he had stormed into the Quebec Major Junior Hockey League with the Halifax Mooseheads. Over two seasons there he racked up 205 points (86 goals, 119 assists), and in his rookie season he was named both the QMJHL and Canadian Hockey League Rookie of the Year. Winnipeg general manager Kevin Cheveldayoff loved what he saw

from Nikolaj on the ice, but also the way the young Dane handled himself off the ice.

"This is a player that every time we had an opportunity to meet with him, we didn't want the interview to end," said Cheveldayoff at the 2014 NHL Entry Draft. "He's going to be an exciting player for a long time."

The Jets selected Nikolaj in the first round of the 2014 NHL Entry Draft. He debuted with the Jets in 2015, and since then, only Blake Wheeler and Mark Scheifele have scored more points in a Jets' sweater than Ehlers. As he heads into his seventh NHL season, he can reflect proudly on how much more diverse his game has become.

"On the defensive side of things, I have been a lot better as my career has gone on," says Nikolaj. "I also got better at shooting the puck more and finding the holes and using my speed to create those holes and shooting lanes."

Looking back, Nikolaj couldn't be happier that he chose hockey over soccer all those years ago. It's a safe bet that Winnipeg fans feel exactly the same way.

DID YOU KNOW?

Nikolaj's dad, Heinz, was taken in the ninth round, 188th overall, by the New York Rangers in the 1984 NHL Entry Draft. Heinz had a long career playing in Europe and Scandinavia, and is now the head coach of Denmark's National Team.

HOCKEY MEMORIES

"I will never forget my first NHL goal. Scoring that, on one of the best goalies of all time, Henrik Lundqvist, in New York, at Madison Square Garden. It was surreal and amazing."

2020–2021 STATS

GP	G	A	PTS
47	21	25	46

Winnipeg Jets' 1st choice, 9th overall, in 2014 NHL Entry Draft
1st NHL Team, Season: Winnipeg Jets, 2015–2016
Born: February 14, 1996, in Aalborg, Denmark
Plays: Left Wing
Shoots: Left
Height: 1.83 m (6'0")
Weight: 78 kg (172 lbs.)

MARC-ANDRÉ FLEURY

Marc-André Fleury has been around the NHL for 18 years and has had to stare down many challenges. But the challenge he faced heading into last season was one of the biggest of his career. He responded by winning the Vezina Trophy as the NHL's top goalie, the first of his career.

After being the number-one goalie for three seasons, Marc-André had been relegated to the back-up role during the 2020 playoffs. Robin Lehner had been picked up in a trade-deadline deal and ended up as the go-to goalie through Vegas's run to the Western Conference Championship series, where they lost to Dallas. Then the Golden Knights extended Lehner's deal by five years. It looked like Marc-André was on the way out. But then Lehner suffered a concussion, and Marc-André, who had been sharing starting duties with his teammate, started 17 of the next 18 games, going 12-5-0 with 3 shut-outs, a .931 save percentage and a 2.02 goals-against average. He played a lot. And when he plays a lot, he plays well.

"When you play all the time, the game feels a little slower," says Marc-André. "Mentally, you don't think as much. You just play the game."

Eventually Lehner got back into the lineup, but Marc-André had made his point: he still had all that it takes to be a number-one goalie in the NHL.

As the seasons roll by, he moves farther up the career wins list. Last season he moved past Ed Belfour and Roberto Luongo into third place in all-time wins. Although he's still well behind Patrick Roy and all-time leader Martin Brodeur, at 691, his 492 wins total is a spectacular accomplishment.

"I was always looking up to Brodeur and Roy. They were always my favorites. I don't really see myself as one of them. I'm just a little dude who plays hockey."

"The wins are very important. It's always been the stat that I looked at the most," says the man teammates call Flower. "If you win, the coach is happy, the players are happy and the fans are happy."

It's a good bet there are many more wins still to come for Marc-André. He can still do it. He proved that last season.

DID YOU KNOW?

In the history of the NHL Entry Draft, only three goalies have been the first pick overall: Michel Plasse (Montreal, 1968), Rick DiPietro (New York Islanders, 2000) and Marc-André Fleury (Pittsburgh, 2003).

HOCKEY MEMORIES

"[My father] would get me dressed at the house in my pads, skates . . . He'd fit me in his truck with everything on and we'd go and wait until the rink opened at six . . . we'd wait by the door so I could practice right away."

2020–2021 STATS

GP	W	L	OT	GAA	SO
36	26	10	0	1.98	6

Pittsburgh Penguins' 1st choice, 1st overall, in 2003 NHL Entry Draft
1st NHL Team, Season: Pittsburgh Penguins, 2003–2004
Born: November 28, 1984, in Sorel, Quebec
Plays: Goaltender
Catches: Left
Height: 1.88 m (6'2")
Weight: 84 kg (185 lbs.)

It was a season where more games were played in fewer days under stranger conditions than at any other time in NHL history. And yet it all came together for Colorado goalie Philipp Grubauer. Philipp had the best season of his NHL career — he started more games, won more, picked up more shut-outs, had his best goals-against average and finished third in voting for the Vezina Trophy as the NHL's best goalie. Along the way, he managed to snag the 100th win of his NHL career. And, as is his nature, he was quick to spread around the credit for his success.

> **"You always have to be alert. Just because you may not get a shot for five or six minutes doesn't mean I can put my umbrella up and hang back in the crease and enjoy the view . . . you've got to be focused and read the situation and be ahead of the play."**

"It's not just one person or a couple of defensemen, it's everybody," said Philipp. "It's taking pride and doing everything the right way, away from the puck, and making the right decisions."

During an important stretch for the Avs in March of last season, Philipp started 14 of 17 games — and won 12 of them.

"I see a whole new level of determination from Gruby," said head coach Jared Bednar last season.

A lot of that determination was directed towards staying healthy. Prior to last season, Philipp had never managed to play in more than 37 games. During the 2019–2020 season he struggled with lower-body injuries and was lost to the team during the second round of the 2020 playoffs.

"He really went to work in the off-season to maintain and strengthen his body so that he was ready to go through the rigors of the season and be a guy we could lean on in a real busy schedule," said Bednar.

Although Philipp had tasted success before in the NHL as part of the 2018 Stanley Cup Champion Washington Capitals, last season's success tasted different. He knew that the season would be shorter and more intense and the pressure would be on him to deliver. He did. And the taste was sweet.

DID YOU KNOW?

Philipp is only the second German-born and trained goalie to win 100 games in the NHL. The first was Thomas Griess. (Olaf Kolzig played internationally for Germany, but he was born in South Africa and grew up in Canada.)

HOCKEY MEMORIES

"We played outside when I was a little kid . . . when the lake froze up in wintertime. It was only about five minutes from my house. My dad was always shooting pucks on the lake or, if there was no ice on the lake, in the backyard."

2020–2021 STATS

GP	W	L	OT	GAA	SO
40	30	9	1	1.95	7

Washington Capitals' 3rd choice, 112th overall, in 2010 NHL Entry Draft
1st NHL Team, Season: Washington Capitals, 2013–2014
Born: November 25, 1991, in Rosenheim, Germany
Plays: Goaltender
Catches: Left
Height: 1.85 m (6'1")
Weight: 85 kg (188 lbs.)

VICTOR HEDMAN

What a wealth of talent the Tampa Bay Lightning have. Andrei Vasilevskiy is one of the best goalies in the world. Up front, veteran Steven Stamkos still possesses one of the finest one-timers in the game. Back of the bench, Jon Cooper, the longest serving head coach in the league, heads into his 10th season. And on the blueline, the Bolts boast one of the most skilled defensemen in the game — Victor Hedman. The Swedish native has been a pillar on the Tampa blueline for a while and stepped into hockey's brightest spotlight during Tampa's last two playoff runs. The 2020 playoffs were the pinnacle as he helped to lead the team to a Stanley Cup and won the Conn Smythe Trophy as playoff MVP. He was also one of the best players on the team when the Bolts repeated as champions last season.

"Your play without the puck is as important as your play with the puck, setting yourself up to have good gaps on guys. When you're facing fast guys like Connor McDavid, it's all about gap control."

"We play a team sport, but if there's one individual trophy that you want to win, then maybe that's the one," says Hedman. "Because if you win that trophy, more times than not, you're winning the Cup."

You'll also find Victor's name on the Norris Trophy, for the NHL's top defenseman.

"For me, he's the best in the league," says Dallas head coach, and former Tampa associate coach, Rick Bowness. "He has size, skating ability, skills. There's nobody who skates like him. He has the ability to control a game."

Another list where you'll find Victor's name at the top is the ice-time (TOI) report after every game. He led the Bolts last season, averaging 25:03 TOI per game. That stat tells you a couple of things: First, he's the best defenseman on the team and that's why he's on the ice more than any other player. But it also tells you that he's in amazing shape. To have the kind of stamina to play those many minutes, night after night, takes a lot of hard work. But hard work is a big part of the identity of the Tampa Bay Lightning. You see it from all the great players on the team. It's what makes them winners.

DID YOU KNOW?

Victor comes from a town in the middle part of Sweden called Örnsköldsvik, which also turned out fellow superstars Daniel and Henrik Sedin, Peter Forsberg, Markus Naslund and Anders Hedberg! Not bad for a town of only 32,000 people.

HOCKEY MEMORIES

"Finally, it's your dream come true. You win the Cup. You don't know what the emotions are going to be, but it was 100 times more emotions than you thought it would be. It's an unbelievable feeling."

2020–2021 STATS

GP	G	A	PTS
54	9	36	45

Tampa Bay Lightning's 1st choice, 2nd overall, in 2009 NHL Entry Draft
1st NHL Team, Season: Tampa Bay Lightning, 2009–2010
Born: December 18, 1990, in Örnsköldsvik, Sweden
Plays: Defense
Shoots: Left
Height: 1.98 m (6'6")
Weight: 109.5 kg (241 lbs.)

PATRICK KANE

Patrick Kane is at the stage of his career when milestone numbers start to show up in the bio. He hit a couple of big ones last season: his 400th goal and, a few nights later, his 1000th regular-season game.

"I'm just really enjoying the game right now. There's numbers you want to reach and stuff, but you really don't think about it much until they come up. I'm just having fun with this group."

"When you start reaching these types of milestones, it leaves you wanting more," said Patrick after that 400th goal. "It's exciting to achieve them and nice to have these types of milestones. Probably means I played a while. I just think that you want to keep getting better and keep trying to help the team as much as you can."

No one has helped the Blackhawks offensively over the last 14 seasons more than Patrick. On October 4, 2007, he stepped onto the ice in Minnesota for his first NHL game. He picked up his first point a couple of nights later, at home, against Detroit. Over the 14 seasons that Patrick has been in the NHL, only Alex Ovechkin (1122) and Sidney Crosby (1103) have racked up more than Patrick's 1088 points. Throw in three Stanley Cup rings, the Calder Trophy as Rookie of the Year, the Conn Smythe for playoff MVP, Hart Trophy (NHL MVP) and Ted Lindsay Award (MVP, voted on by the players) and you have a strong case for Patrick being regarded as one of the greatest of his era.

He was also a bit of a trailblazer. When he was drafted, Patrick was slightly on the small side for an NHL forward. However, what he lacked in size he made up for with his staggering skill set — his skating, passing, shooting and on-ice vision were all off the charts. His success paved the way for other smaller, skilled forwards we see in today's game: players like Johnny Gaudreau and Mitch Marner.

Four hundred goals, over 1000 games. How many more seasons does Patrick have in him?

"I always think there is room in my game to get better. There will always be things you can do to better the team or better yourself," says Patrick.

An even better Patrick Kane? I'll bet that's a scary thought if you have to play against him.

DID YOU KNOW?
Patrick's son, Patrick Timothy Kane III, was born in November 2020. "We tried to put a hockey stick in his hand, but he wasn't having it too much. Maybe he won't like hockey, who knows? We'll let him play whatever he wants to."

HOCKEY MEMORIES
"If there were 365 days in a year, I was probably on the ice for 350 of them. That was my childhood and that's what I loved to do . . . I played other sports too, but nothing really compared to playing hockey."

2020–2021 STATS

GP	G	A	PTS
56	15	51	66

Chicago Blackhawks' 1st choice, 1st overall, in 2007 NHL Entry Draft
1st NHL Team, Season: Chicago Blackhawks, 2007–2008
Born: November 19, 1988, in Buffalo, New York
Plays: Right Wing
Shoots: Left
Height: 1.78 m (5'10")
Weight: 80.5 kg (177 lbs.)

MITCH MARNER

Mitch Marner was a highly touted junior player, then a first round draft pick. He was talked about in glowing terms in his first few seasons, he led the team in scoring last season and now he is one of the most admired players on the Toronto Maple Leafs. Through it all there has been one constant: hard work.

> "It's been a drastic change from my first year to now. I realize that I have to be a leader on this team, to be vocal . . . try to be a guy that can be leaned on in any situation."

"I'm always motivated. I always want to be doing better, I always want to be better," says Mitch. "I think that's kind of the motto for our team — everyone wants to be better, everyone wants to be the best that they can be. So, I just try to go out there and do my part of that and make sure I'm ready to play every game."

Teammates will tell you that one of the biggest things he brings to the team is a great attitude. "I've always been the type of guy to try to bring positive vibes," says the guy teammates call Mitchy.

For all great athletes, the season never really ends. You might be able to take a week or two off after the playoffs, but pretty soon it's back to training. With the level of play in the league as high as it has ever been, you have to be in game shape from day one of training camp. That's why you would have seen Mitch, just days after the Leafs were knocked out of the playoffs in 2019, out in his neighborhood running wind sprints to work on his endurance. That hard work paid off last season as he played the best hockey of his career, mostly on a line with veteran Joe Thornton and his pal Auston Matthews.

"Mitch is the total package for sure," says Matthews. "He's got the skills to make high end plays, but it's his hockey IQ that separates him from the other players. The way he reads the game offensively/defensively is elite."

Heading into his sixth season, Mitch is hoping to reach the next stage of his NHL journey — a run towards a Stanley Cup championship. After last year's early playoff exit, he and his teammates will have plenty of motivation.

DID YOU KNOW?

Mitch is the first player in Toronto Maple Leafs history to start his career with five straight 40-plus assist seasons.

HOCKEY MEMORIES

After he got his first NHL paycheck, Mitch and his mom, Bonnie, headed to a car dealership. Imagine the smile on his mom's face when he told her the car was for her, as a way of saying "thanks" for all the time she spent driving him to games and practices when he was a kid.

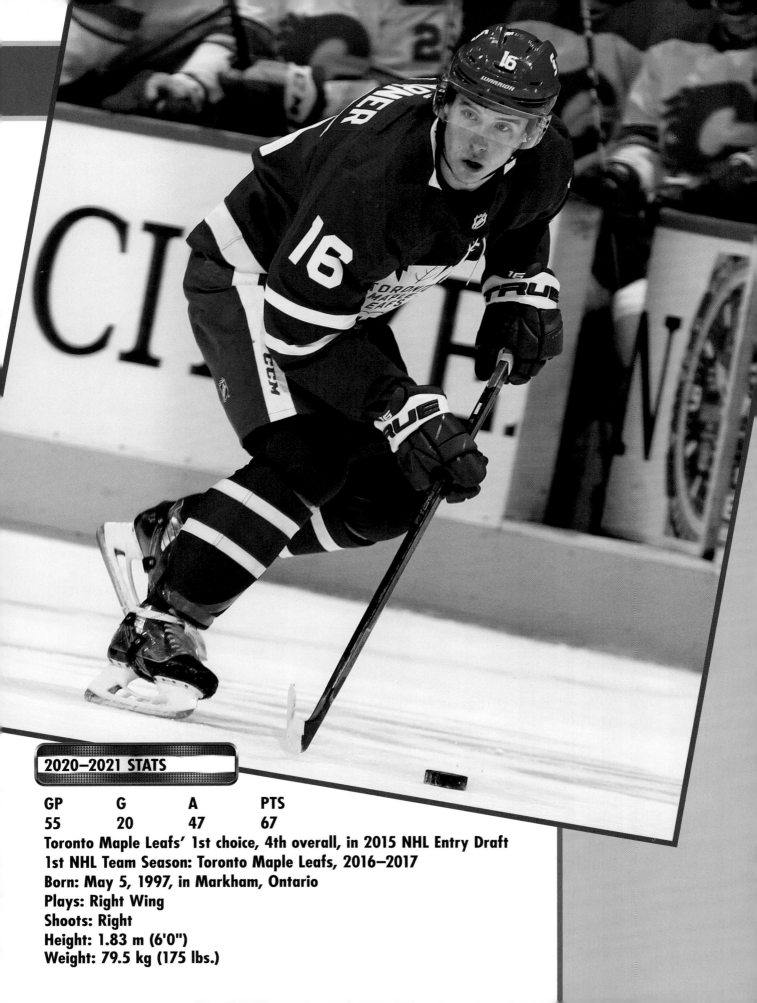

2020–2021 STATS

GP	G	A	PTS
55	20	47	67

Toronto Maple Leafs' 1st choice, 4th overall, in 2015 NHL Entry Draft
1st NHL Team Season: Toronto Maple Leafs, 2016–2017
Born: May 5, 1997, in Markham, Ontario
Plays: Right Wing
Shoots: Right
Height: 1.83 m (6'0")
Weight: 79.5 kg (175 lbs.)

TORONTO MAPLE LEAFS

The 2020–2021 NHL season was definitely weird: a shorter schedule, playoffs going deep into the summer and the league sectioned off into American and Canadian divisions, with teams not mixing until the playoffs. But if you make your living as an NHL player, you learn to adapt and roll with whatever gets thrown at you as best you can.

"To me, hockey means everything. It's what I've done my whole life. I'm very fortunate to be living the dream and playing in the NHL."

"We all thought it was going to be exciting to play in the Canadian Division," said Auston before the start of last season. "With the teams from the west, normally you don't get to see them much. Playing them 9 or 10 times . . . it'll make some rivalries between teams and players. It should be some good hockey."

There certainly was some good hockey. In fact, there was some great hockey — especially from Auston. He was also right about the rivalries, especially against Connor McDavid and the Oilers. Auston raised his already great game to an even higher level, leading the NHL with 41 goals — an average of .79 per game, by far the highest of his career.

However, things didn't go well in the playoffs for Auston and his teammates. Despite holding a three games to one lead in their opening-round series against the Montreal Canadiens, they lost in seven games. Auston managed only one goal in the series.

"I hold myself to a high standard. To not produce the way I wanted to is obviously frustrating. I think it's probably the mental side. It's realizing when you've got a team in that position to get the job done and close them out. That's what great teams do and we failed to execute in that department. There's no excuses. You've got to make your own luck."

The best players bounce back from playoff heartbreak stronger than ever. Count on another big season from Auston.

DID YOU KNOW?

Auston played baseball and hockey while growing up in Arizona. Some say he was even better at baseball than hockey. What made him go all in on hockey? His dad says that Auston found "there was just too much standing around in baseball."

HOCKEY MEMORIES

Auston's first NHL game, on October 12, 2016, was one for the memory banks. With his parents in attendance, he scored four goals on the Ottawa Senators, "It was pretty special having my parents there to share the moment with me."

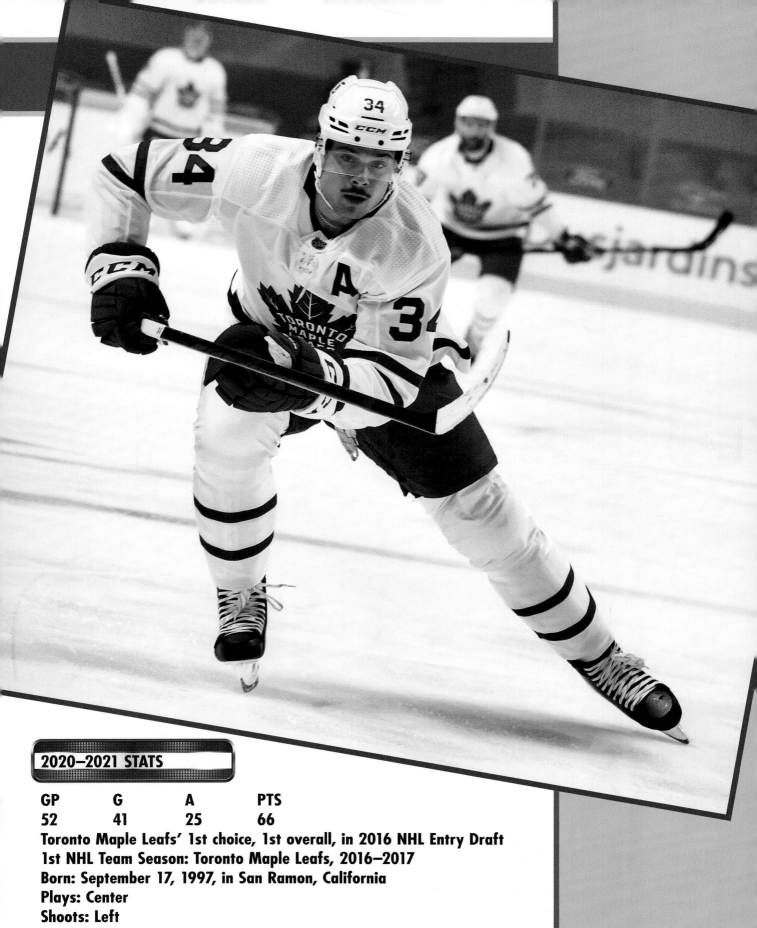

GP	G	A	PTS
52	41	25	66

Toronto Maple Leafs' 1st choice, 1st overall, in 2016 NHL Entry Draft
1st NHL Team Season: Toronto Maple Leafs, 2016–2017
Born: September 17, 1997, in San Ramon, California
Plays: Center
Shoots: Left
Height: 1.90 m (6'3")
Weight: 100 kg (220 lbs.)

CONNOR McDAVID

When you've been a hockey phenom since you were barely in your teens, not much about your life is normal. Like, for example, getting a phone call from Wayne Gretzky while you're out with some teammates.

"It was my first year playing junior hockey and I was in the car with my roommate," recalls Connor. "The music was going and I answer my phone, and it's like, 'Hi, Connor. It's Wayne Gretzky.' I remember saying, 'Turn the music down!' It was the weirdest thing. I thought I was being punked."

As it turned out, there was no punking going on. Gretzky was calling to congratulate him on some milestone he had achieved in the OHL. The Great One was offering congratulations to Connor again last season, when Connor reached the 500 career points mark. It took him only 369 games to get there. That's not quite as fast as Gretzky, who hit that mark in an NHL-record 234 games, but it did match the pace of Connor's boyhood hero, Sidney Crosby.

Connor remembers the first time he got to play against Crosby. He had to wait until his second NHL season because he'd been injured both times the Oilers played the Penguins during his rookie season.

"We were in Pittsburgh and I remember watching him the whole time during the anthem and thinking to myself: 'That's Sidney Crosby over there, and I'm going to get to play against him.'

"There's been quite a few players that get to 500, but to do it as fast as he's done it and in the company that he's done it with is pretty remarkable."
— Edmonton coach Dave Tippett

While last season was yet another great individual one for Connor — he led the league in scoring for the third time in his career, was unanimously voted the winner of the Hart Trophy as the NHL MVP and won the Ted Lindsay Award as the most outstanding player in the league — it didn't come with a long run in the playoffs or a shot at the Cup. That left a very sour taste.

"We're a group that expects more from ourselves. We want to push and continue to grow and, obviously, we didn't do that in the playoffs ... The regular season doesn't mean anything."

DID YOU KNOW?
Connor is the proud owner of a Bernedoodle named Lenny. The two even make a cameo appearance in a music video for the song "A Few Good Stories" by Brett Kissel and Walk Off The Earth.

HOCKEY MEMORIES
As a kid, Connor spent a lot of time in the car with Mom or Dad, driving to and from games. "We had some great conversations in the car," says Connor's mother, Kelly. "If something didn't go right, you had the drive home to kind of work through it and talk about it."

2020–2021 STATS

GP	G	A	PTS
56	33	72	105

Edmonton Oilers' 1st choice, 1st overall, in 2015 NHL Entry Draft
1st NHL Team, Season: Edmonton Oilers, 2015–2016
Born: January 13, 1997, in Richmond Hill, Ontario
Plays: Center
Shoots: Left
Height: 1.85 m (6'1")
Weight: 87.5 kg (193 lbs.)

DARNELL NURSE

Family can have a big impact on what you decide you want to do when you grow up. For example, look no further than Darnell Nurse. He was surrounded by athletes and the spirit of competition from the day he was born, so it's no surprise to see him making a living as an NHL player.

"Our family is so tight . . . everyone keeps in touch. So if you're going through something, you've got that ability to reach out and find out what someone else might do if they were in this situation or that situation."

Darnell's dad played in the CFL and his mom played university basketball. His uncle Donovan McNabb was a star quarterback in the NFL. Basketball is his sisters' sport: Kia in the WNBA and on Canada's National Team and Tamika on the Junior National Team. Darnell's cousin Sarah plays on Canada's National Women's Hockey Team.

Maybe things were a little competitive around the Nurse household?

"Everything we did was always competitive," recalls Kia. "We'd play one-on-one [basketball] or shoot hoops to see who had to do the dishes. Darnell sometimes got me shooting hoops, but I usually beat him in the one-on-one games."

These days, at least when it comes to hockey, it's rare to see Darnell getting beaten one-on-one. He's developed into one of the best young defensemen in the NHL. If it's an important moment in the game, you're likely to see him jumping over the boards. And if there's an important issue to be discussed, you're likely to hear Darnell's voice. He's one of the leaders on the Oilers. For example, his determination to help make the offensively oriented team a little more accountable defensively carried a lot of weight.

"Everyone loves goals, right? But it's the defensive part of the game that will always be a big part of winning in the playoffs," said Darnell. "Look at a team like Tampa. They're known for scoring goals, but in the playoffs they can play a tight checking game as well as anyone."

You know that when the competition gets notched up, Darnell will be there. He's been surrounded by it since he was a kid.

DID YOU KNOW?
If he had to pick another sport, Darnell says it would be football. "I'm not very good at basketball. I've played some lacrosse. But football has always been a sport that I've loved. I'd love to be a quarterback."

HOCKEY MEMORIES
In 2013 Darnell was cut by the Oilers at training camp and sent back to play another year of junior hockey. He was also cut from Canada's National Junior Team that year! But looking back, Darnell knows it made him mentally tougher and a better player in the long run.

GP	G	A	PTS
56	16	20	36

Edmonton Oilers' 1st choice, 7th overall, in 2013 NHL Entry Draft
1st NHL Team Season: Edmonton Oilers, 2015–2016
Born: February 4, 1995, in Hamilton, Ontario
Plays: Defense
Shoots: left
Height: 1.93 m (6'4")
Weight: 100 kg (221 lbs.)

MARK SCHEIFELE

It's fair to say that pretty much every NHL player loves the game, and it's also fair to say that there aren't many who love it as much as Winnipeg superstar Mark Scheifele.

> "I'd love to be a general manager one day because I've always wanted to be that guy who feels like he could mesh a team together."

"There is not a waking moment when I'm not thinking about hockey," says Mark. "Behind family, hockey is definitely the most important thing in my life."

Mark's knowledge of the game and the tendencies of other players and teams is encyclopedic. He can tell you what the pattern of an opponent's stick is, how they like to set up their power play and maybe even who the last guy off the ice during warm-up is. Winnipeg fans will know that Mark always has to be the last player off the ice for the Jets, and he often tries to wait out players on the other team at the end of warm-up to make sure he's the last guy off the ice, period.

"It's just a weird little thing I have, that's kind of developed," Mark says with a smile. "I've just kind of stuck with it. I just like to get in a few extra touches of the puck."

Whatever Mark is doing, it works. He led the Jets in scoring again last season, as he has for three of the last five, and reached the 500 career points mark during a game against the Calgary Flames on May 5, 2021, with an assist on teammate Blake Wheeler's goal — Wheeler's 800th career point.

One of the nicest things about Mark is that he takes none of what he has for granted. He works hard, for sure. But he knows how lucky he is.

"To be able to play the game we love on a day-to-day basis, and have it as our job . . . playing that game that we all grew up loving? It's the little kid in all of us."

And, like any little kid, the ultimate dream is lifting the Stanley Cup up over his head on the final day of the playoffs.

"I try to put my best foot forward, every game, every season," says Mark. "If I do that, that gives our team a better chance to get to that ultimate goal."

DID YOU KNOW?
Mark strives to keep his language clean, on or off the ice. "If I was ever to say a curse word in front of my mom, she'd lose her mind."

HOCKEY MEMORIES
The NHL returned to Winnipeg in 2011, when the Atlanta Thrashers were relocated. The new Winnipeg Jets' first draft selection was Mark Scheifele. "I can remember it like it was yesterday. Definitely one of the best moments of my life," recalls Mark.

2020–2021 STATS

GP	G	A	PTS
56	21	42	63

Winnipeg Jets' 1st choice, 7th overall, in 2011 NHL Entry Draft
1st NHL Team, Season: Winnipeg Jets, 2013–2014
Born: March 15, 1993, in Kitchener, Ontario
Plays: Center
Shoots: Right
Height: 1.90 m (6'3")
Weight: 94 kg (207 lbs.)

TIM STÜTZLE

Tim Stützle entered the world on January 15, 2002, in Viersen, Germany, a small town on the western edge of the country. Exactly 19 years later he stepped onto the ice in Ottawa to make his debut as an NHL player. He had already come a long way on a journey that was just getting started.

Tim began the season as the youngest player in the NHL, but his play didn't reflect that. In fact, there were nights when he was the best player on the ice.

"Every game and every shift, I get more comfortable. I feel more confident to make plays."

"He's dangerous out there," said Ottawa coach D.J. Smith. "He's going to be a first line power play type guy for a long time. It's amazing to me that he's doing it this soon. For his age, it's unbelievable what he's doing out there."

Tim was selected by the Ottawa Senators as the third overall pick in the 2020 NHL Draft. He was drafted out of the top German hockey league (DEL) rather than from a Canadian junior team. Playing in the top league in Germany with Mannheim meant that Tim was playing with, and against, many veteran professional players.

"I was able to learn an incredible amount playing in the DEL with Mannheim," says Tim. "I think maybe I was a step further than playing another year against juniors somewhere else."

Last year was another long one for Ottawa Senators fans. The team showed moments of promise, but struggled for much of the season and finished in second-last place in the North Division. Since the team's trip to the Eastern Conference Final in 2017, the Sens haven't played a post-season game. However, watching Tim develop as the season went on gave fans a reason to be hopeful. He looked more comfortable offensively and, importantly for a young player, defensively as well. He's on a journey towards being one of the best players in the NHL, and Sens fans are thrilled to be along for the ride.

DID YOU KNOW?

When Tim was selected by Ottawa at the 2020 NHL Entry Draft, his name wasn't called out by the team's general manager. Instead, it was announced by *Jeopardy!* game show host, and University of Ottawa graduate, Alex Trebek.

HOCKEY MEMORIES

Tim played for Germany at the 2021 World Junior Hockey Championships and he made the most out of his appearance. He was selected as the best forward of the tournament — the first time a German player ever received the honor.

2020–2021 STATS

GP	G	A	PTS
53	12	17	29

Ottawa Senators' 1st choice, 3rd overall, in 2020 NHL Entry Draft
1st NHL Team, Season: Ottawa Senators, 2020–2021
Born: January 15, 2002, in Viersen, Germany
Plays: Left Wing
Shoots: Left
Height: 1.85 m (6'1")
Weight: 85 kg (187 lbs.)

ANDREI VASILEVSKIY

Looking at past NHL draft selections, it becomes clear who was a good pick and who wasn't. In the 2012 NHL Entry Draft, Andrei Vasilevskiy was Tampa's second choice in the first round, 19th overall. But none of the 18 players who went before has enjoyed the same level of success. There have been some good, solid players — Alex Galchenyuk, Morgan Rielly and Filip Forsberg — but the man teammates call Vasy was a steal at number 19 because he's been better than good. He's been great. Many would say he is the best goalie in the NHL right now. If the class of 2012 were re-drafted today, there's no question who the number-one pick would be.

> "When you see him get into the zone, where every save is so easy and even the difficult ones look easy, we just try to stay out of his way and let him do his thing."
> — Tampa captain Steven Stamkos

"Just from a pure talent standpoint, he's the best goalie in the league," said former NHLer and television commentator Brian Boucher. "Some people have talent and never live up to expectations. He's lived up to expectations."

Andrei is heading into his sixth season as the number-one goalie with Tampa. He won the Vezina Trophy in 2019, and has led the league in wins for the last four seasons. Since 2016-2017, when Vasy became a starter, no goalie in the NHL has won more games than his total of 172.

"Just to watch his growth over the last few seasons, it's been awesome to see," said Tampa head coach Jon Cooper.

Andrei was particularly awesome during a stretch last spring when he reeled off a franchise-record 12 consecutive wins. He also shone brightly in the playoffs and was voted the Conn Smythe Trophy winner as the post-season MVP.

"He's such a big part of our team and sometimes, but not too often, you have to rely on him to keep us in the game when we're not at our best," said teammate Victor Hedman. "He's been tremendous all season."

Tremendous last season and, quite likely, for many years to come. The Tampa scouting staff have made some great draft selections over the years, but snagging Andrei back in 2012 may be one of their best. Lightning struck on that day.

DID YOU KNOW?
Andrei was the first goalie in Tampa franchise history to win the Vezina Trophy, and only the second Russian-born goalie to win it. The first was Sergei Bobrovsky, who won in 2013 and 2017.

HOCKEY MEMORIES
"I played forward a couple of years when I was 8 or 9 years old, but I told my dad that it was too tough to be skating that much and I wanted to stay in the blue paint and make saves."

2020–2021 STATS

GP	W	L	OT	GAA	SO
42	31	10	1	2.21	5

Tampa Bay Lightning 2nd choice, 19th overall, in 2012 NHL Entry Draft
1st NHL Team, Season: Tampa Bay Lightning, 2014–2015
Born: July 25, 1994, in Tyumen, Russia
Plays: Goaltender
Catches: Left
Height: 1.90 m (6'3")
Weight: 102 kg (225 lbs.)

SHEA WEBER

Like all regular-season NHL games in Canada last season, the one between the Montreal Canadiens and the Vancouver Canucks on February 2, 2021, was played in an empty arena. In this case, that was a little sad because it meant that Shea Weber played the 1000th game of his career in front of an audience of empty seats. But that was life in the NHL last season, and Shea, famous for his level-headed approach to the game and life, kept things in perspective.

"You grow up as a kid loving it, that's why you play it. That's why we still play it. That's what it's all about. Just coming to the rink and being with the guys and play the sport you love the most."

"These are circumstances no one really could have predicted and there are people in a lot worse places. So, just kind of looking forward to getting it over with and playing," said Shea the day before the game.

Shea has had an amazing career. Teammates and opponents alike point to him as one of the greatest defensemen of his era. He leads all active NHL defensemen in career goals (224) and power-play goals (106).

He won an Olympic gold medal with Canada in 2010 and has been named a First or Second Team All-Star four times. Surprisingly, Shea has never won the Norris Trophy as the NHL's top defenseman.

"I think he could've won it, but I don't think he's the kind of guy that's upset he didn't," says fellow NHL defenseman and friend Marc-Edouard Vlasic. "The guy is all about team championships. He'd rather win one Stanley Cup than ten Norris Trophies . . . that's just the type of player he is."

His attitude, perhaps more than anything else, is the reason he's so widely respected around the league. He works harder than anyone on the team and he leads by example.

"It's special," said Shea about reaching 1000 games. "As a kid, you dream of playing in the NHL. Realistically, it's a lot tougher than people realize . . . so just making it here has been really special. Having a career this long and of this many games is something I never really imagined."

DID YOU KNOW?

Shea has one of the hardest shots in hockey. In fact, at the 2010 Olympics he fired one right through the net. It wasn't until play stopped a few seconds later that referees reviewed the video and awarded Canada the goal.

HOCKEY MEMORIES

Shea's approach to the game is something he credits to his mom and dad. "Neither of them took a day off . . . My dad would work all day, 10-hour shifts, come home and coach me and my brother or both. I can't say enough."

2020–2021 STATS

GP	G	A	PTS
48	6	13	19

Nashville Predators' 4th choice, 49th overall, in 2003 NHL Entry Draft
1st NHL Team, Season: Nashville Predators, 2005–2006
Born: August 14, 1985, in Sicamous, British Columbia
Plays: Defense
Shoots: Right
Height: 1.93 m 6'4")
Weight: 104 kg (229 lbs.)

REFEREE SIGNALS

Do you know what is happening when the referee stops play and makes a penalty call? If you don't, then you're missing an important part of the game. The referee can call different penalties that result in anything from playing a man short for two minutes to having a player kicked out of the game.

Here are some of the most common referee signals. Now you'll know what penalties are being called against your team.

Boarding
Checking an opponent into the boards in a violent way.

Charging
Checking an opponent in a violent way as a result of skating or charging at him.

Cross-checking
Striking an opponent with the stick, while both hands are on the stick and both arms are extended.

Elbowing
Checking an opponent with an elbow.

High-sticking
Striking an opponent with the stick, which is held above shoulder height.

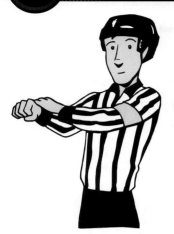

Holding
Holding back an opponent
with the hands or arms.

Hooking
Using the blade of the stick
to hold back an opponent.

Icing
Shooting the puck across
the opposing team's goal
line from one's own side
of the rink. Called only
if the opposing player
touches the puck first.

Interference
Holding back an
opponent who does not
have the puck in play.

Kneeing
Using a knee to hold
back an opponent.

Misconduct
A ten-minute penalty — the
longest type called. Usually
for abuse of an official.

Roughing
Shoving or striking an opponent.

REFEREE SIGNALS

Slashing
Using the stick to strike an opponent.

Spearing
Poking an opponent with the blade of the stick.

Slow whistle
The official waits to blow his whistle because of a delayed offside or delayed penalty call. Done while the opposing team has control of the puck.

Tripping
Tripping an opponent with the stick, a hand or a foot.

Unsportsmanlike conduct
Showing poor sportsmanship toward an opponent. For example: biting, pulling hair, etc.

Wash-out
Goal not allowed.

FINAL TEAM STANDINGS 2020–2021

North Division

Team	GP	W	L	OT	PTS
TORONTO	56	35	14	7	77
EDMONTON	56	35	19	2	72
WINNIPEG	56	30	23	3	63
MONTREAL	56	24	21	11	59
CALGARY	56	26	27	3	55
OTTAWA	56	23	28	5	51
VANCOUVER	56	23	29	4	50

West Division

Team	GP	W	L	OT	PTS
COLORADO	56	39	13	4	82
VEGAS	56	40	14	2	82
MINNESOTA	56	35	16	5	75
ST LOUIS	56	27	20	9	63
ARIZONA	56	24	26	6	54
LOS ANGELES	56	21	28	7	49
SAN JOSE	56	21	28	7	49
ANAHEIM	56	17	30	9	43

East Division

Team	GP	W	L	OT	PTS
PITTSBURGH	56	37	16	3	77
WASHINGTON	56	36	15	5	77
BOSTON	56	33	16	7	73
NY ISLANDERS	56	32	17	7	71
NY RANGERS	56	27	23	6	60
PHILADELPHIA	56	25	23	8	58
NEW JERSEY	56	19	30	7	45
BUFFALO	56	15	34	7	37

Central Division

Team	GP	W	L	OT	PTS
CAROLINA	56	36	12	8	80
FLORIDA	56	37	14	5	79
TAMPA BAY	56	36	17	3	75
NASHVILLE	56	31	23	2	64
DALLAS	56	23	19	14	60
CHICAGO	56	24	25	7	55
DETROIT	56	19	27	10	48
COLUMBUS	56	18	26	12	48

GP = Games played; W = Wins; L = Losses; OT = Overtime losses; PTS = Points

Top Ten Points Leaders 2020–2021

	PLAYER	TEAM	GP	G	A	P	S	S%
1	CONNOR McDAVID	EDMONTON	56	33	72	105	200	16.5
2	LEON DRAISAITL	EDMONTON	56	31	53	84	168	18.5
3	BRAD MARCHAND	BOSTON	53	29	40	69	143	20.3
4	MITCH MARNER	TORONTO	55	20	47	67	156	12.8
5	PATRICK KANE	CHICAGO	56	15	51	66	191	7.9
6	AUSTON MATTHEWS	TORONTO	52	41	25	66	222	18.5
7	MIKKO RANTANEN	COLORADO	52	30	36	66	177	17
8	NATHAN MacKINNON	COLORADO	48	20	45	65	206	9.7
9	MARK SCHEIFELE	WINNIPEG	56	21	42	63	126	16.7
10	SIDNEY CROSBY	PITTSBURGH	55	24	38	62	159	15.1

GP = Games played; G = Goals; A = Assists; P = Points;
S = Shots; S% = Percentage

Top Ten Goalies — Total Wins 2020–2021

	PLAYER	TEAM	GP	W	L	OT	SV%	GA	GAA
1	ANDREI VASILEVSKIY	TAMPA BAY	42	31	10	1	0.925	93	2.21
2	PHILIPP GRUBAUER	COLORADO	40	30	9	1	0.922	77	1.95
3	MARC-ANDRÉ FLEURY	VEGAS	36	26	10	0	0.928	71	1.98
4	TRISTAN JARRY	PITTSBURGH	39	25	9	3	0.909	100	2.75
5	CONNOR HELLEBUYCK	WINNIPEG	45	24	17	3	0.916	112	2.58
6	JACOB MARKSTROM	CALGARY	43	22	19	2	0.904	111	2.68
7	JUUSE SAROS	NASHVILLE	36	21	11	1	0.927	78	2.28
8	MIKE SMITH	EDMONTON	32	21	6	2	0.923	71	2.31
9	VITEK VANECEK	WASHINGTON	37	21	10	4	0.908	95	2.69
10	SEMYON VARLAMOV	NY ISLANDERS	36	19	11	4	0.929	72	2.04

GP = Games played; W = Wins; L = Losses; OT = Overtime and/or Shut-Out Losses;
SV% = Save percentage; GA = Goals Against; GAA = Goals-Against Average

END-OF-SEASON STATS

Countdown to the Cup 2021–2022

EASTERN CONFERENCE

STANLEY CUP FINAL

CONFERENCE FINAL

ROUND TWO

ROUND ONE

THE CHAMPION:

WESTERN CONFERENCE

CONFERENCE
FINAL

ROUND
TWO

ROUND
ONE

NHL AWARDS

Here are some of the major NHL awards for individual players. Fill in your selection for each award and then fill in the name of the actual winner of the trophy.

HART MEMORIAL TROPHY
Awarded to the player judged to be the most valuable to his team. Selected by the Professional Hockey Writers Association.

2021 winner: **Connor McDavid**

Your choice for 2022: _____

The winner: _____

ART ROSS TROPHY
Awarded to the player who leads the league in scoring points at the end of the regular season.

2021 winner: **Connor McDavid**

Your choice for 2022: _____

The winner: _____

CALDER MEMORIAL TROPHY
Awarded to the player selected as the most proficient in his first year of competition in the NHL. Selected by the Professional Hockey Writers Association.

2021 winner: **Kirill Kaprizov**

Your choice for 2022: _____

The winner: _____

JAMES NORRIS TROPHY
Awarded to the defense player who demonstrates throughout his season the greatest all-round ability. Selected by the Professional Hockey Writers Association.

2021 winner: **Adam Fox**

Your choice for 2022: _____

The winner: _____

VEZINA TROPHY
Awarded to the goalkeeper judged to be the best. Selected by the NHL general managers.

2021 winner: **Marc-André Fleury**

Your choice for 2022: _____

The winner: _____

TED LINDSAY AWARD
Awarded to the most outstanding player in the NHL as voted by members of the NHL Players' Association.

2021 winner: **Connor McDavid**

Your choice for 2022: _____

The winner: _____

MAURICE RICHARD TROPHY

Awarded to the player who scores the highest number of regular-season goals.

2021 winner: **Auston Matthews**

Your choice for 2022: _____

The winner: _____

WILLIAM M. JENNINGS TROPHY

Awarded to the goalkeeper(s) who played a minimum of 25 games for the team with the fewest goals scored against it.

2021 winners: **Marc-André Fleury and Robin Lehner**

Your choice for 2022: _____

The winner: _____

LADY BYNG MEMORIAL TROPHY

Awarded to the player judged to have exhibited the best sportsmanship combined with a high standard of playing ability. Selected by the Professional Hockey Writers Association.

2021 winner: **Jaccob Slavin**

Your choice for 2022: _____

The winner: _____

FRANK J. SELKE TROPHY

Awarded to the forward who best excels in the defensive aspects of the game. Selected by the Professional Hockey Writers Association.

2021 winner: **Aleksander Barkov**

Your choice for 2022: _____

The winner: _____

CONN SMYTHE TROPHY

Awarded to the player most valuable to his team in the Stanley Cup playoffs. Selected by the Professional Hockey Writers Association.

2021 winner: **Andrei Vasilevskiy**

Your choice for 2022: _____

The winner: _____

BILL MASTERTON MEMORIAL TROPHY

Awarded to the player who best exemplifies the qualitites of perseverance, sportsmanship and dedication to hockey. Selected by the Professional Hockey Writers Association.

2021 winner: **Oskar Lindblom**

Your choice for 2022: _____

The winner: _____

FUTURE STARS?

The first player taken in the NHL Entry Draft doesn't always turn out to be the best player from the draft. In 2011, the 58th player taken was Tampa forward Nikita Kucherov. Ten years later, Kucherov has more career points than any other player taken in that draft. The first overall pick, Edmonton's Ryan Nugent-Hopkins, is sixth on that list. You just never know.

Here are a few players from the class of 2021 who we think are good bets for success.

Owen Power

Mason McTavish

OWEN POWER
Defense
1.98 m (6'6") / 96.5 kg (213 lbs.)
Born: November 22, 2002, in Mississauga, Ontario
2020–2021 Club: University of Michigan Wolverines, NCAA

MASON McTAVISH
Center
1.85 m (6'1") / 94 kg (207 lbs.)
Born: January 30, 2003, in Zurich, Switzerland
2020–2021 Club: EHC Olten, SL (Swiss League)

WILLIAM EKLUND
Left Wing
1.78 m (5'10") / 80 kg (176 lbs.)
Born: October 12, 2002, in Haninge, Sweden
2020–2021 Club: Djurgården IF, SHL (Swedish League)

KENT JOHNSON
Center
1.85 m (6'1") / 75 kg (165 lbs.)
Born: October 18, 2002, in North Vancouver, British Columbia
2020–2021 Club: University of Michigan Wolverines, NC